"Queen Liliuokalani"

The Hawaiian Kingdom's Last Monarch, Hawaii History

A Biography

Kale Makana

Although the author and publisher have made every effort to ensure that the information in this book was correct at press time, the author and publisher do not assume and hereby disclaim any liability to any party for any loss, damage, or disruption caused by errors or omissions, whether such errors or omissions result from negligence, accident, or any other cause.

Edition v2.00 (2019.10.30)

Special thanks to the volunteer readers who helped with proofreading. Thank you so much for your support.

Introduction

The 1800s, particularly the latter half of that century, was a time full of change, orchestrated chaos, and new beginnings. England was in the throes of the Industrial Revolution. North America, primarily the United States of America, was blazing a trail for the western half of the country. In addition to exploration of the continent, the country broke out in a civil war over the matter of states' rights. South America was in a sort of Cultural Revolution as they drifted away from the control of Spain and their governments were ruled by military dictators. Economically, they were reluctant to grow with the world's economy. Asia found itself losing many of its Chinese population to California's gold rush and was wrestling with the fact that the nations have been grappling with the concept of British rule for quite some time. Yet, located in the center of Pacific Ocean, a string of islands existed making waves in World History comparable to any other much larger country or nation. This string of islands is referred to today as Hawaii.

The first settlers of Hawaii are believed to be the Polynesians that came on double-hulled canoes from New Zealand, Tahiti and other nearby countries in search of whatever exploration brought them. They did not come empty handed as they brought livestock, elephant ears, domestic animals, and other plant life.

Geographically speaking, the islands were formed from molten lava, or magma, that came from the volcanic eruptions. Over time, the magma would flow and add layer after layer upon itself as it cooled and hardened. As time progressed, these layers eventually broke above the water's surface of the Pacific Ocean and continued. As with all developing lands, an ecosystem later developed. For the longest time, until the first settlers, only birds and plants lived on the islands. Mammals did not inhabit the islands until humans brought them along.

Anthropologically speaking, to take a glimpse at the early villages in Hawaii, one would see that religion and the ancient kapu system was very important. The first structures in each village on each island were usually the temples. From there, they would build the buildings that housed the royal possessions. The last buildings were usually those of the commoners. The myths of the origins of the islands held a strong foothold in the beliefs of the islanders all the way until the latter nineteenth century, though some still practice the art of storytelling and passing along the legends today.

Chapter One

The Polynesians believed that the origin of Hawaii came from the god Pele. It has been said that Pele followed a star that began in the northeastern part of the sky, which was brighter than the others. Pele migrated toward the bright star. As Pele did this, she awoke one morning to discover that the air was filled with a scent of something she recognized. She looked into the distance and saw a mountain standing high above the horizon—its peak hidden by a haze of smoke. She decided that this place would be her new home. This new home was called Hawaii.

She walked up the mountain with her magic stick that she called "Pa'oa." There, she found a part of the earth had collapsed in on itself. She called this Kilauea. Unfortunately, there was another god living on the beautiful mountain. This god was named Ailaau. Both Ailaau and Pele wanted to keep Kilauea for their home, so they fought over it. There was a lot of damage done as a result of this fight, but at the end of the day, Pele was victorious. The people of the island loved Pele.

After a while, Pele began to dream. In her dreams, she saw a man named Lohi'au. He was the chief of the island of Kaua'i. Pele sent her sister, Hi'iaka, to bring this chief back to her. However, she told her sister that she only had forty days in which to complete this task. If she failed to come back in that time, she would punish her sister and kill her friend, Hopoe. As Hi'iaka reached the island if Kaua'I, she discovered the Lohi'au was dead. Refusing to fail in her task, she brought the chief back to life and began the journey back to Kilauea.

The trip back to Kilauea took longer than anticipated. Pele began to think that her sister had fallen in love with the man from her dreams. Jealousy took over as she caused an eruption that turned Hopoe into a stone statue. Once Hi'iaka returned, she found that Hopoe had been turned into stone and became filled with rage. She led Lohi'au to the edge of the crater where she knew that her sister would see, and she embraced Lohi'au. The jealousy-filled Pele covered Lohi'au with lava.

After all was said and done, and the anger subsided, the two sisters became filled with a great sadness. Pele lost the love of her life and Hi'iaka lost her friend, Hopoe. So, Pele decided to bring Lohi'au back to life again and let *him* decide whom he loved. As she did that, he chose Hi'iaka. So, Pele sent them along with her complete blessing and the pair sailed back to the island of Kaua'i.

The islanders, to this day, still say that the goddess Pele lives on the island of Hawaii ruling over the volcanoes. She shows that she still resides by the smell of Sulphur and her lava, which flows building a new island to the south. This island is still submerged under the water and is named Loahi.

From the soul that was captured in the myth, the archipelago that is known as the Hawaiian Islands have evolved from a simple piece of land settled by a seafaring people to a unified kingdom thanks to Kamehameha the First. In 1810, Kamehameha the First, united the Hawaiian Islands into one kingdom. He did not do this alone. With the help of foreign weapons as well as advisors, he was able to make it happen. Kamehameha's birth was prophesied as him being a great leader, and it was said that he would defeat all his rivals as well as reign supreme over all the islands. Alapai ordered that the baby prince be put to death, but instead someone too him and watched him grow, giving him the name Kamehameha, which means "the very lonely one" or "the one set apart."

Once Kamehameha had united the islands into one kingdom, the monarchy adopted a flag. It was similar to the flag that Hawaii uses now. The top corner next to the flag pole is eight horizontal strips changing between white, red and blue to represent the eight major islands.

After Kamehameha the First died, he left the throne to his son Prince Liholiho, who became Kamehameha the Second. From the moment he assumed control, he was pressured by his mother to abolish the "kapu system" which had ruled life on the islands as far back as their own history told. Liholiho showed this change by sitting down to eat dinner with his step-mother and other women of chiefly rank. Eating with females was a forbidden act under the old system.

Kapu is another way to refer to ancient Hawaiian code of conduct. The system was universal in lifestyle, gender roles, politics and religion as well as others. Breaking a law or regulation of Kapu even unintentionally a lot of times ended in immediate death. Kapu in English means "forbidden".

The line of succession eventually passed to a young princess named Lydia Liliʻu Loloku Walania Wewehi Kamakaʻeha. She was also known as Lydia Kamakaʻeha Pākī (her Christian name) and Liliʻoukalani was her chosen Royal name. Her husband was John Owen Dominis. He was born in America, then later became the Prince consort to the Kingdom of Hawaii once he was married to Liliʻuokalani.

Chapter Two

John Dominis was born to Captain John Dominis and Mary Lambert Jones. Mary Lambert Jones' parents were Owen Jones and Elizabeth Lambert. John Dominis,Sr. was sent to America in 1819. He came from Trieste during the Napoleonic Wars. The Dominis family came from Italy. More specifically, the Dominis family can trace its origins to the Dalmatian island of Arbe. John Owen Dominis' father, also John Dominis worked for Josiah Marshal of Boston, Massachusetts. The years passed and sometime in 1831, John and his wife moved to Schenectady, New York. The following year, their son, John Owen Dominis, was born in March of 1832.

John Owen Dominis' childhood was not uncommon of the times. His father was a sea captain, which meant that they moved from port to port. Five years later, he did just that. In 1837, John Dominis, Sr. moved his family all the way from New York to Hawaii. They left their daughters behind at boarding school in New York, but unfortunately, the two girls died soon after.

By the time this happened, King Kamehameha III decided to award the family a settlement that included land as part of a lawsuit filed by the British Consul Richard Charlton. Never giving up his "sea legs", the captain continued to accept positions taking voyages so that he could build his family a larger house. One of these voyages included one to China in 1846, which he sailed for China on the Brig *William Neilson*. The purpose of this voyage was to purchase Chinese-made furniture for the house that was almost done. This voyage would be John Dominis' last voyage as the ship was lost at sea, and he was presumed dead. Now, Mary was considered a widow and left to raise the younger John Owen Dominis alone. To support herself, she would rent a suite of rooms in the home her husband built. The first of these boarders was a man named George Brown who later dubbed the home "Washington Place." For a while, as you will later see, it was used as a governor's residence. Today, it is a museum dedicated to Hawaii's unique history.

Growing up, John Owen Dominis attended a day school that was run by Mr. and Mrs. Johnston. This school sat next to a school that was strictly for the native Hawaiian nobility. It was during that time at the day school that he met Princess Lydia Kamaka'eha Paki. At that time, he never paid any particular attention to her.

In time a corial relationship developed and John courted Lili'uokalani for two years. On September 16, 1862, the pair finally said their vows after several delays—one of which was due to the death of Prince Albert, the son of Kamehameha IV.

The marriage was more of a marriage of convenience. It was customary for a young woman of a certain social status or financial position in life to marry "well", and it was no different for Lili'uokalani. John would often socialize without her. They also had no natural children of their own as Lili'uokalani could not have children. She did, however, accept the child John Dominis had as a result of an extra-marital liaison with a woman named Mary Purdy. Mary Purdy was a servant to Lili'uokalani. This child's name was also named John Dominis, but Lili'uokalani adopted him and called him 'Aimoku. Young Aimoku Dominis was born on January 9, 1883. This was not the only time that John Dominis was unfaithful to his wife, but it was accepted as a fact of life by Lili'uokalani.

Another child that Lili'uokalani raised through *hanai* tradition was the daughter of Luther Aholo. Aholo was a private secretary of John Dominis when he was appointed to the position of governor of Maui. He was also a native Hawaiian. In addition to Aholo, a man by the name of Abraham Fornander was often left in charge during Dominis' absence. He was also an advisor to the Queen.

Aholo's second wife was pregnant, but he had lost other children to illness with his first wife. Lili'uokalani was distressed over what to do—as was a natural feeling considering she existed in a time when there was great change in her home and change was tearing the fabric of the old ways. She explained to her advisor, Fornander, that she discussed the matter of adopting Aholo's child and keeping with tradition. However, her husband not only disagreed, but was angry at the suggestion of the idea.

The thing was is that her brother's wife was also pregnant, but her brother often changed his mind as he feared losing his line of succession. It was *that* child that Lili'uokalani would have actually raised in accordance with ancient tradition, but he did end up changing his mind. He sent his sister on a trip to, as he claimed it, better her health. Upon her return, she learned that Aholo's wife had actually died after giving birth to her daughter. Without her husband's approval or knowledge, Lili'uokalani went directly to the island and claimed the female child as her own and raised her in *hanai* tradition. That child was named Lydia Kaonohiponiponiokalani Aholo.

13

Chapter Three

The Origins of Lili'uokalani.

On September 2, 1838, Caesar Kapa'akea and Anale'a Keohokalole gave birth to a precious baby girl. This girl child was no ordinary baby. She would become a pivotal figure in Hawaii's history. She was born near the Punch Bowl on the island of Oahu. Caesar and his wife also had a son, who later came to be known as King Kalakuaua.

Keohokalole was born in 1816 as the daughter of the High Chieftess named Kamaokalani and the High Chief who was called Aikanaka. Her lineage traces back to both Kame'eiamoku and Keawe-a-Heulu who both supported King Kamehameha the First.

At that time, tradition among Hawaiian royals was to marry those to whom you were related—particularly cousins. So, in 1833, she married Caesar Kapa'akea who was the son of a lesser ranking chief. Through their marriage, they had ten children: David, James, Lydia, Anna, Kaiminaauao, Miriam and Leleiohoku. Having so many children was not abnormal as many children did not survive to adulthood due to diseases and such.

After she married Caesar Kapaakea, her paternal grandmother and great uncle gave her many parcels of land. Despite the amount of land she had, she was still poor in actual cash on hand. This caused her to have to sell off her land in order to maintain the household's necessary finances.

Caesar Kapa'akea himself was also of noble blood, as previously mentioned. He was born a year earlier than his wife in Maui. There were many spellings for his name, but most of history recognizes the Christian form of "Ceaser." However, for posterity, we will stick with "Caesar", which is a mixture of the Christian and Hawaiian form.

Caesar Kapa'akea's father was Chief Kamanawa II and his mother was Chieftess Kamokuiki. He, too, was able to trace his lineage to one of the five Kona chiefs who supported King Kamehameha the Great. Though his family, at the time of his marriage to his wife, was considered high-ranking at first, their rank was decreased when his father was hanged for the murder of his mother.

It was in 1835 that he married his wife, High Chiefess Analea Keohokalole. It was a sacred union due to their familial relation as first cousins. By the time of his wife's death, only four children remained in good health.

One of his children was Lili'uokalani. Because he was a high ranking chief at the time, but as per tradition, he sent all ten of his children to be raised by other nobles. His daughter, Lydia Lili'uokalani, was sent to be raised by Abner Paki and Laura Konia. As she grew under the supervision of Abner Paki and Laura Konia, she eventually came to attend the Royal School. It was there that she was taught a firm grasp of the English language, music arts, and geography as she would travel often during the course of her childhood. Lili'uokalani developed a keen sense of pride for her Hawaiian ancestry, its traditions and its people.

Abner Paki married his first wife, Chieftess Kuini Liliha. Because their marriage produced no children, however, he later married Kamehameha III's niece named Laura Konia. She was the daughter of Kamehameha III's half-brother. An interesting fact is that the wedding between Paki and his second wife was the first Christian ceremony that was performed on the islands for those who were native to the islands. The wedding took place in December of 1828.

After they were wed, Konia and Paki lived at the capital near King Kamehameha III and the Premier Kekauluohi. One time, a merchant by the name of Gorham Gilman visited Paki and his wife at their home. He wrote in his journal about how welcoming they were, especially the children. He noted that Konia referred to him as her "keiki", or "child" as translated to English. He also noted how the port town was always filled with whaling ships and their families who desired to spend their wintertime in at the tropical port. His journal entry gave a great insight into what life was like at the end of the nineteenth century in Hawaii.

He also details some physical traits of Paki as a tall man who was also incredibly strong. He outlines a situation in which he was told about where Paki held a team of frightened horses at bay. Imagine what strength that was required to do so!

Konia did have a daughter of his own. Her name was Bernice Pauahi Paki. Following the tradition of *hanai,* he gave up his daughter to Kina'u, who was the Premier of Hawaii. The purpose of *hanai* was to strengthen familial bonds, but the Christian missionaries compared it to giving away puppies. They abhorred the practice and said that families should not do that. Yet, the practice continued despite their opinions on the matter. Later on, Bernice was married off to the son of the Premier, Prince Lot.

This tradition of marrying one's relatives had been a long-standing one throughout the islands among the natives. However, Bernice was headstrong. She did not want to marry Prince Lot as she was not "in love" with him. Despite being told that it was her duty repeatedly, she ended up marrying an American man by the name of Charles Reed Bishop. It would be many years later before there was a reconciliation between Paki and his daughter, Bernice.

Though Paki did not raise his own daughter, Bernice, due to these traditions, he did raise Lydia Lili'uokalani. Since she was raised in the Paki household, she was often referred to as Lydia Paki. She grew up in Honolulu in Paki's house, which was also named Hale'akala. This was roughly translated to "House of the Sun", though the house was actually pink in color and not the actual color of the sun.

In regard to Lili'uokalani's birth parents, Caesar Kapa'akea served on both the House of Nobles and the Privy Council in Hawaii under Kamehameha III, Kamehameha IV, and Kamehameha V. When he died in November of 1866, he was buried at Kawaiaha'o Cemetery but later moved to the Royal Mausoleum of Hawaii nine years later.

By the time her mother died, however, only half of the land bequeathed to her remained. Yet, it had to be split four ways among the surviving children. Those four children were David, William, Miriam, and Lydia Lili'uokalani.

David later became king in less than twenty years later. He had no personal wealth, but this lack of money eventually led to his acceptance of bribes and accusations of corruption. Many scandals about such activities swept through the islands during his short reign.

Chapter Four

As Lili'uokalani grew up, she eventually came to marry a man by the name of John Owen Dominis. Her marriage was described in great detail in her book about her life *Hawaii's Story by Hawaii's Queen* (recommend follow-up reading to this book). She introduces the chapter about her marriage by detailing the events of the death of her father-in-law, Captain Dominis. She does mention that he was not happy at the homestead at Washington House, but perhaps his dissatisfaction came from the fact that he was a "traveler." He did not like being tied down to any land. Captain Dominis was a seafaring man and needed the ocean like it needed the waves. So, she begins with his last voyage in 1846 in which he was never heard from again.

She continues to detail how distraught her mother in law is about her husband's death. She maintains a hope, but slowly resigns herself to the fact that her husband is not going to come back. Rather than fully resign to the stages of grief, Lili'uokalani's husband, John Owen Dominis, became a focal point. Her mother in law began to obsess in gaining her son's attentions and affections.

Queen Lili'uokalani notes that, for all intent and purposes, John Owen Dominis was an only child despite the existence of two older daughters who had died earlier. In her book, she commented on how her husband was so devoted to his mother. For a while, she admired the devotion. It was quite endearing. Yet after a while, she sensed that she was viewed as an intruder in the relationship of mother and son. The forced realization of this caused a lot of grief in her marriage. She wrote about how though John Owen Dominis was kind and caring toward her (his wife), he would not intervene in any situation in which his mother's feelings might become injured. She noted that it was almost until the latter years of the old woman's life that she came to realize that Lili'uokalani had chosen to resign to this unspoken arrangement between the three of them.

Lili'uokalani also talks about how she and her husband were invited to visit Prince Lot and Mr. and Mrs. Robert Davis on a trip to the main island of Hawaii. At this time, Prince Lot was nearly reaching his turn at the throne of Hawaii as Kamehameha V. Such pleasant days occurred often, but at infrequent times.

At the time of history that this all took place, there were no hotels on any of the islands. Can you imagine what Hawaii or any of the islands that existed in the chain looked like with absolutely ZERO hotels? It must have been spectacular! At this point in the book, Lili'uokalani began talking about how the Kings and Chiefs of the past always took proper care of the needs of his subjects. In return for that care, the subjects always saw to the bounty of the tables of the royal families. She compared that idea and tradition to how the people erected homes for the royals to stay in at the time of her life rather than simply providing food. Those "homes" were like hotels of modern day.

Lili'uokalani talked about the homes that Prince Lot owned all over Hawaii and some of the other islands. She comments on the hospitality of the Hawaiian people. I suppose that if one were astute, he or she could compare it to the belief of "Southern hospitality" in the mainland United States. Even the chiefs which hailed from the ancient families welcomed any stranger into their homes for hospitality, as was the custom.

On was on this trip in 1862 that she noted that there was a younger contender for the throne, though Lili'uokalani wrote in her book that this younger brother did not live to the age in which he could have assumed control as regent. She also speaks of Princess Ruth and "lady's confinement." In this particular day in age, that usually meant that it was almost time for Princess Ruth to give birth and would be confined to her room. Something unusual was noted. Prince Lot told Lili'uokalani to break tell Princess Ruth that she should break with *hanai* tradition, though the child had already been promised to Princess Ruth's cousin, Mrs. Pauahi Bishop. Prince Lot said that because he was deprived of the love of his mother and treated as a stranger in the home he was adopted into, that the child of Princess Ruth should be raised by its mother and not a relative.

As one could imagine, something of this magnitude—a royal ordering that tradition be broken—was not taken lightly. Because Princess Ruth did not follow the orders of the soon-to-be Kamehameha V, Prince Lot signed an executive order that removed the child from all interest in Princess Ruth's property. Of course, this was all a waste of time as the child in question later died at the age of six months.

In November of 1863, Lili'uokalani notes in her book that Kamehameha IV passed away after only reigning for nine years. His wife, Queen Emma, refused to return to any kind of public life. It was now time for Prince Lot to assume the throne as Kamehameha V. He would be the last of the Hawaiian monarchs to carry the name of "Kamehameha."

Lili'uokalani went on to detail how Prince Lot, now Kamehameha V, showed favor to John Owen Dominis. At this point, Kamehameha V appointed

Dominis as his confidential adviser, private secretary, and even was appointed governor. Though this appointment of governor usually came with a time in office of four years, Lili'uokalani said that the position was always renewed without question.

Being married to Lili'uokalani had its other advantages for John Owen Dominis as well. He was Royal Commander of the Royal Order of Kamehameha, the Royal Commander of the Royal Order of Kalakaua, as well as other orders. He was also appointed to the Privy Council, the House of Nobles and ruled as Governor of O'ahu. He was on the Board of Health, the Board of Education, the Bureau of Immigration and Quartermaster General and Commissioner of Crown Lands. He was also appointed, from 1878 to 1886, as the Royal Governor of Maui. After his term as Royal Governor or Maui ended, he became the Lieutenant General and Commander in Chief.

Lili'uokalani was proud of her husband's achievements, but as a member of the royal family, that did not mean she was left without responsibilities of her own. Her brother King Kalakaua left her in charge in 1881 while he took a trip around the world. During this time, a terrible outbreak of smallpox occurred in Hawaii. Many Hawaiians, who had no natural immunity to the disease, died. As it turned out, the Chinese laborers who came over to work in the fields were the source of the disease. Lili'uokalani made the executive decision to close the ports. Many of the sugar farm owners were against the move as it had a negative effect on their business, but Lili'uokalani's concern was for her people. She firmly believed that it was her place to look after the interests of her people above the interests of someone's business.

Chapter Five

Influencial Events in Hawaiian History

The McKinley Tariff Act of 1890

In 1876 William McKinley, ran and was later elected to sit in Congress as the Republican Party's expert on how the protective tariff could bring prosperity. His time in Congress and understanding of the current economic situation of the country led to his 1890 McKinley Tariff. His ideas for this tariff were quite the controversy at the time. The Democrats attempted to gerrymander, or rezone the districts for the purpose of creating a political stronghold, and were subsequently successful. Yet, his tariff was passed.

The McKinley Tariff, in short, rose the tariff rates to fifty percent for manufactured American products. There were many items, such as sugar and coffee, which no longer carried a tariff, though. This tariff also allowed the United States to circumvent the need for approval from Congress in raising duties to match foreign rate hikes.

Farmers in America suffered because the tariff raised prices of farming equipment at a time in which the prices of agriculture were on the decline. In the latter part of the nineteenth century, there was very little competition for American farmers from the produce that was imported, but the tariff created a more violent competition in the market.

As far as trade, the tariff was reduced for many foreign products in exchange for a reduction on tariffs for American exports. There was a provision in the McKinley Tariff Act called the "Blaine-Harrison Reciprocity Provision" that allowed this. Basically, it was a type of "quid pro quo" between Congress and foreign governments. James Blaine used this provision to take advantage of the bargaining power of the President of the United States in order to gain access to Latin American markets and expand American trade. While this sounds like a great thing on the whole, this had a negative impact on many American farmers who were still reeling from the rise in prices on machinery needed in order to run their farms.

In regard to the American people as a whole, the tariff caused prices to rise everywhere. Basically, the items one could purchase from overseas increased in price as opposed to the local products that were similar in comparison more so than the locally produced products; however, those local products also increased on price due to the cost of the equipment used to fabricate. Without giving an extensive lesson on macroeconomics and microeconomics, this change meant that the concept of what a 'livable wage' was changed. The amount of money earned by an employee for his time to fabricate these goods would have to go up to compensate for the decreased purchasing power as well as the increase in expenses incurred by the average American at the time.

By the time 1875 came, fifteen years prior to the enactment of the McKinley tariff, Secretary Hamilton Fish had already sponsored a reciprocity treaty with the Hawaiian Islands. This made it possible for the owners of the sugar plantations on Hawaii to have more control over trade of one of their primary exports at the time. By the time the McKinley Tariff Act of 1890 took dominance over the markets, the American market was flooded with competition from overseas sugar markets. This led directly to a decline in the economy of Hawaii and created many political issues between the Queen's supporters and the planters. This also set the stage for what was to soon happen next.

The Republican Party was in power of Congress in 1890 when the McKinley Tariff Act was passed, despite its lack of popularity. Because of the lack of popularity as well as the negative effect it was having on the world markets and the dissatisfaction of the citizens, especially in the United States of America, the Republicans were defeated in both the House and the Senate in the next elections of 1892. In addition to losing the House and the Senate, the Republican Party also lost the presidency to a Democrat by the name of Grover Cleveland. Yet, it would be the Republican ideals that caused the Hawaiian monarchy to fade into the wind.

Chapter Six

Before Lili'uokalani was named Queen, her brother, Kalakaua, ruled. He did leave his sister in charge on occasion, and it was he who favored her husband. When he decided to travel the world to study other monarchs and just to experience the world, he left her in charge. His travels took him from San Francisco, California to Japan, China, Burma, Italy, Belgium, Germany, Austria-Hungary, France, Great Britain, Ireland, and other places all before returning to his home of Hawaii. It was during this trip that he met with many of the heads of state in each country. This trip was not only important because of the exposure the Kingdom of Hawaii gained, but it was important because Kalakaua was the first monarch to travel the globe in such a fashion. As a matter of fact, he was even presented with the Royal Order of Vasa Grand Cross by Sweden's King Oscar II.

In 1882, he built the 'Iolani Palace, which cost a hefty sum of $300,000. It was furnished with articles ordered from Europe during Kalakaua's trip around the world.

Kalakaua ordered a statue made of Kamehameha I to celebrate the unification of the Hawaiian Islands. Interestingly, the ship carrying the first statue sank near the Falkland Islands. So, Kalakaua had to order a replacement statue. This statue was unveiled in 1883.

King Kalakaua was quite ambitious, but his ambition stood out in his time. Had he reigned in earlier centuries, his desire to begin a Polynesian Empire might have succeeded. However, with expansionism and the California Gold Rush happening not far off on the other side of the Pacific Ocean, he was unsuccessful due to the Bayonet Constitution that was put into place the following year.

By the time 1887 rolled around, many of the Caucasian settlers on Hawaii were growing irritated with Kalakaua and his reign. The census was that the increased debt and financial hardships felt by the elites on the islands were directly attributed to his rule. Some did want to place his sister, Lili'uokalani, on the throne in his place while others wanted to annex the islands into the United States of America. Those who desired the latter created an organization called the Hawaiian League. In June of 1887, the stormed the Iolani Palace and forced Kalakaua to sign a new constitution that they drafted under duress.

This new "constitution", later called the "Bayonet Constitution", essentially removed the primary weight of control and power from the monarchy. In this "constitution", many restrictions were placed on rights that many had taken for granted such as voting rights. Essentially, over three-fourths of native Hawaiians found themselves unable to vote due to the restrictions to gender, property, age, and literacy requirements. This made it to where mostly those who were Caucasian or in the upper class were allowed the vote. Many of these same upper-class citizens also "found" themselves in high-ranking government positions, giving the elite primary control of government functions. The sole purpose of the Bayonet Constitution was to disenfranchise the native Hawaiians and shift the power toward those with European and American ancestry. In addition to the disenfranchisement of the native Hawaiians who were not in the "elite" class, the Bayonet Constitution also allowed the legislature, also run by Europeans and Americans due to the overthrow of the monarchy, the power to override a veto by the King as well as restraining the King from making decisions or taking action without the cabinet's approval.

The legacy of Kalakaua's reign and life was not a bad one, though history recorded by his adversaries would attempt to make it out to be so. He was nicknamed the "Merrie Monarch" because he was known to always be quite happy and enjoyed life. He also brought back the practice of hula dancing as it had previously been banned in 1830 by Queen Ka'ahumanu after she became a Christian. He also brought back many of the other "forbidden" arts such as martial arts, luau, and surfing. They were originally banned because they were celebrations to other gods.

Kalakaua was also credited with writing the song called *Hawaii Ponoi,* which is currently the Hawaiian state song.

In January of 1891, Kalakaua passed away. This left his sister, Lili'uokalani, as the reigning monarch, though she would have very little power due to the "Bayonet Constitution." Her husband, John Dominis, would be declared Prince Consort.

Chapter Seven

After her brother died in January of 1891, Lili'uokalani became Queen. Unfortunately, her reign would be short, but it would seem that she and her brother would have the greatest impact on their tiny kingdom since King Kamehameha the Great.

The McKinley Tariff Act of 1890, just the year before Lili'uokalani assumed the throne, was the source of a major recession on the Hawaiian Islands since the primary export of Hawaii at the time was sugar, one of the items directly affected by the McKinley Tariff Act of 1890. The Hawaiian League, one of two factions against the monarchy, wanted to have Hawaii considered for annexation into the United States of America in order to re-stabilize the market. However, in late 1893, Queen Lili'uokalani drafted a new constitution to override the Bayonet Constitution and restore the monarchy's control. However, John Stevens, the American minister in Hawaii along with United States Marines from the *USS Boston*, stormed Iolani Palace as well as other government controlled buildings. By 1894, he officially deposed Queen Lili'uokalani and placed a provisional government in control.

Once President Cleveland, who was elected into office of the United States of America in 1892, realized that the Hawaiian people stood behind their dethroned Queen, he attempted to make what he felt was a good compromise. If Lili'uokalani granted amnesty to those involved in the coup of her kingdom, he would place her back on the throne as if nothing had ever happened. However, it did not work out this way. At first, she refused. Then, she changed her mind and agreed to the terms. Yet, the provisional government denied her reinstatement and placed Sanford Dole as its president of the territory.

As one could imagine, this angered Lili'uokalani greatly. Over the next year, she plotted to take back her kingdom and her throne by planning a counterrevolution. She stored firearms at her home for this purpose, but the existence of the firearms was discovered. She was arrested in 1895, but she adamantly denied knowledge of the firearms or how they got there and was later released. In three more years, Hawaii would become annexed by the United States of America as a territory.

Queen Lili'uokalani's Incarceration

Queen Lili'uokalani's sentence for planning a counter-revolution was that she pay five thousand dollars and hard labor for a term of five years. She details in her autobiography that this sentence was not actually carried out. She believes that the government of the United States or the "figurehead" government put into place in Hawaii never intended to execute at all. History would be more inclined to agree with her as well as the fact that it was more for show and to humiliate her in front of her people, yet the love her people had for her did not waver for the most part.

Very few things actually changed during her imprisonment. She was still allowed writing paper and pencils, though she was not allowed newspapers or other books that might encourage her resistance. It was during this imprisonment that she wrote *Aloha Oe* as well as other songs. She was still allowed to walk around the veranda, though under the watchful eye of a sentry. She was also allowed to receive gifts from friends.

In addition to the pleasures of her pre-incarcerated life, she was also fed just as she was before with very delectable meals. In her autobiography, she mentions many of the ladies who served her house during this time and praises them for their kindness. Also, she discusses how though everything sent to her was searched by the guards, only the newspapers that had anything to do with government were held away from her.

She continues to discuss that in June of 1895, she became slightly anxious. Rumors of her release flew around, but no results were yielded. Her health was on the decline, but her regular doctor was in San Francisco at the time. Two months later, she still found herself incarcerated. Worse yet, an epidemic of cholera had broken out.

Yet, in only a month, Queen Lili'uokalani would find that those rumors of a release would come true as she was released September 6 of 1895. At this time, she was sent to Washington Home, which was the place she had lived at earlier in her adult years. Though she was released, she was placed on a sort of "parole." She was given a custodian, sixteen servants, and no longer allowed to have any gatherings at her home or attend gatherings of any group of people. This meant that she was also not allowed to attend a church.

Her custodian, Mr. Charles Wilson, was a strange man. In her autobiography, Lili'uokalani notes that she did not particularly like Mr. Wilson, but appreciated his sentiment in regard to his keeping of strangers from entreating themselves upon her private life.

In February of 1896, Lili'uokalani writes that she was having dinner with Mr. Wilson's wife and Mr. Kamakau. She was delivered the papers of her release from parole as prisoner with the condition that she not leave the island of Oahu.

In December of 1896, Lili'uokalani was granted permission by President Dole, the figurehead of Hawaii for the interim government, to visit Boston. She enjoyed her visit, but there, she was told by some of the ladies in the area that they were rooting for her cause. These ladies believed that Hawaii should be ruled by Hawaiians. At this point, Lili'uokalani was gracious for their ideals, but her health caused her to pause with concern in regard to how much "fight" was left in her.

As one continues to read her story from her perspective, she details her trip to Washington the next month in 1897. Two particularly important men accompany her on her trip from Boston, Massachusetts to Washington, D.C-- Mr. Joseph Heleluhe and Captain Julius Palmer. hough Captain Palmer was brought to Hawaii as a "pet" of sorts of those who ran the provisional government who sought annexation, he decided to investigate the matters himself and form his own opinion. That opinion just happened to coincide with Queen Lili'uokalani. Captain Palmer believed that the Hawaiians should be allowed to choose their own government and also that Queen Lili'uokalani's constitutional rights should be restored. He was important to her mission to speak with the President of the United States at the time in seeking to present her case to those in government.

After President Grover Cleveland called for an investigation into her overthrow, he called on Congressman James Henderson Blount to do the investigating. In Blount's report, he did conclude that the representatives sent to Hawaii by the United States government abused their power. President Cleveland offered a treaty to Lili'uokalani in order to restore her power that also gave amnesty to those who overthrew her. She refused, but also, Dole refused Cleveland's demands to reinstate Lili'uokalani to her rightful position.

However, a report done by Senator John Tyler Morgan, who happened to be in favor of annexation, discredited Blount's report. This action stopped Cleveland's efforts to re-instate the queen. It would be over one hundred years before Hawaii would ever receive even an apology from the United States government. This "apology" was signed by President Bill Clinton on the one hundredth anniversary of the overthrow of Queen Lili'uokalani.

Financially, the reason for the annexation was that American farmers and sharecroppers who lived in Hawaii sought a way to avoid paying American tariffs during the exporting of their crops to the mainland. As mentioned before, the McKinley Tariff Act of 1890 caused a lot of backlash for many countries who did regular business with the United States.

By 1897, William McKinley became President of the United States. In July of 1898, Hawaii became an official territory of the United States of America via the Newlands Resolution. None of the native Hawaiians attended the ceremony at Iolani Palace. The ones who did happen to leave their home did so in silent protest by wearing the country's flower or flag on their person. Most, however, refused to leave their homes— including Lili'uokalani. The date of August 12, 1898, the Hawaiian flag was lowered and the Hawaiian national anthem was played for the final time. Many native Hawaiians shed tears for their lost country as they resigned themselves to the fact that their beloved country was lost to the hands of the greedy.

By 1898, though, several different groups who were against the annexation signed petitions to seek to have the original government restored. They eventually became known as the "Hawaiian Independent Party" and elected Robert Wilcox as a representative from what was now known as the "Territory of Hawaii."

Chapter Eight

Queen Lili'uokalani, now just Lili'uokalani of Hawaii, withdrew from public life in 1899 after the events that transpired since the Bayonet Constitution.

The Hawaiian Organic Act was passed soon after Queen Lili'uokalani withdrew from the public eye in 1900.

In 1917, Lili'uokalani passed away after problems arising from a stroke. She left a legacy of her own, though her monarchial powers were limited. She had quite an impact on her people as she was fiercely loyal to them. She used her power and influence on those who ruled before her to try to ensure that certain traditions were upheld by the monarchy.

However, her legacy was more than just a political one. She was quite the accomplished musician and poet having penned several songs and poems that simply told her own story. Her most well-known songs, however, are *Aloha Oe* and *The Queen's Prayer*.

Her song, *Aloha Oe*, is one of Hawaii's four national anthems. The song was written about two lovers who must depart and bid each other farewell. It has many romantic notions and other variations, but the common link is that it was inspired as Queen Lili'uokalani witnessed a tender farewell given by a man named Colonel James H. Boyd.

The Queen's Prayer was written by Queen Lili'uokalani after she was arrested for her counterrevolution attempt when stockpiled weapons were discovered at her home. She wrote it as a way, or so it is said, to cope with the arrest and come to a certain level of "peace" and forgiveness of the illegal seizure of her throne by the interests of the American and European businessmen.

Queen Lili'uokalani also wrote a story titled, *Hawaii's Story by Hawaii's Queen*. It is her autobiography written in 1898, nineteen years before she suffered a stroke and passed away. In her book, she outlines everything from her childhood to her coming into power as Queen as well as from her points of view on the overthrow of the monarchy and how she was lied to by the United States of America as the provisional government refused her to retake the throne when she agreed to Cleveland's terms.

Though this was her autobiography, many historians view this as one of most important sources of information as they study the overthrow of the Hawaiian monarchy. History, of course, is often reported by the victors in any situation. For example, the Morgan Report and the Native Hawaiians Study Commission Report of 1893, which disavow any interference or responsibility of the United States of America or Grover Cleveland's involvement in the overthrow of the Hawaiian monarchy, disagree with the events told by Lili'uokalani in her autobiography, but much of what she has said is plausible. Regardless, however, of whether people *believe* everything outlined in Lili'uokalani's book, it certainly cannot be denied that this was her way to vent her frustration of the circumstances that would eventually lead to the death of a kingdom.

Conclusion

The tale of Lili'uokalani is one that can only be told with the breath from the winds of the Hawaiian Islands as the sound of waves crashing upon the shore, the drum of the hula, and the sound of a quiet Hawaiian evening under the stars echoes in the background. Only then can a person truly understand the life of the last ruling monarch of the Kingdom of Hawaii. Only then can a person truly grasp the level of love and adoration she had for her people and her people for her.

The Queen had a tenacity about her that was not entirely uncommon through history, but yet, it was still unique to the person she was raised to be. The mantra she practiced for her life was "E onipa'a I ka 'imi na'auao" or in English, it is translated as "Be steadfast in the seeking of knowledge." Queen Lili'uokalani was most definitely that, if nothing else. She sought knowledge everywhere she was in every aspect of her life. She had a great thirst for life as did her predecessor and brother, Kalakaua. As a matter of fact, the standard for the family was a burning torch, which signified a lasting flame.

Perhaps to truly understand her dedication to her people, we should let the beloved Hawaii Queen explain her beliefs herself. She speaks of her people— the native Hawaiians—who have been through so much in their history on the islands. She talks about how she feels the desire of the mainland United States to annex the tiny kingdom is merely a way to defraud the native people of their birthrights. She continues on to write about her extreme dislike for the European and American settlers as they claim themselves as "Hawaiians." In her eyes, they will never been true Hawaiians as they are only "aliens" in her eyes.

In addition to the over one hundred and fifty works written by her, she also translated the Hawaiian Creation Chant titled, *Kumulipo*. She did this also while she was incarcerated for her failed counterrevolution attempt to reclaim her throne. The phrase itself translates into "a source of darkness." To Hawaiian culture, "darkness" is simply considered a place where creation takes place rather than something to fear. Instead, it is revered.

According to the *Kumulipo*, it took what was known as one "cosmic night" to create the entire world. A "cosmic night" is many nights over time. In essence, this is like a combination of the "creation through evolution" theory some Christian scientists believe. The *Kumulipo* would be recited during the season in which the god Lono was celebrated, which is also known as the *makahiki* season. Since Lili'uokalani had literally nothing but time during her imprisonment, she translated all two thousand one hundred and two lines of the *Kumulipo*.

More on the Kumulipo

There are sixteen sections that make up the *Kumulipo*. Each of these sections is called a "wa." The first "wa" through the seventh "wa" occur under the cover of darkness and do not happen in an actual "physical" realm. It is actually believed to happen in a spiritual plane.

The first, second, and third "wa" include sea and air life such as sea urchins (in the first), fish (in the second) and birds (in the third "wa"). For every sea creature, there is a supposed land creature that is a distant cousin, according to this concept. For example, a frigate or the Hawaiian Noddy Tern is related to a goose or owl.

The fourth through the seventh begin introducing the creation of more complex life such as complex plant life like bamboo as well as lizards, turtles, jellyfish, taro, fleas, rats and dogs. By the end of the seventh "wa", the "darkness" began to dissipate and the physical realm begins to emerge as the eighth "wa" introduces the four major divinities, which are as follows: La'ila'i (Female), Ki'i (Male), Kane (God), Kanaloa (Octopus).

The ninth "wa" outlines the birth of mankind as La'ila'I and Ki'I mate. From La'ila'i's brain, man emerges. However, it does not end there. The tenth "wa" outlines how La'ila'i grew tired of Ki'i and then decided to mate with her other brother, Kane. With Kane, she bore four additional children. After that, she returned to Ki'i and had three more children for a total of eight children. The eleventh through sixteenth "wa" traces the ancestry and pays homage to many of the other original tribes of Hawaii.

If one were to compare the *Kumulipo* to the King James Version of the Bible, one would see the similarities between it and the book of Genesis as it outlines the family lines from Adam and Eve through the ages to the great kings of the area.

Feminism and Women's Rights

Queen Lili'uokalani was also not like many other women of her time who simply sat by and allowed the men to lead her thoughts or her actions. She was quite intelligent and very legal minded. In her autobiography, she details how she signed her married name of "Liliuokalani Dominis" to the document she was forced to sign when she was to agree to Cleveland's terms. However, her argument was that she had never *legally* assumed her husband's last name. It was only assumed that she had done so because it was Christian tradition for the wife to take the husband's last name. Yet, she had not done so and writes the statement that there never has been anyone by the name of "Liliuokalani Dominis" on any legal document.

Using this argument, she filed a lawsuit under the Fifth Amendment seven years before her death. The Fifth Amendment of the Constitution of the United States is as follows: "No person shall be held to answer for a capital, or otherwise infamous crime, unless on a presentment or indictment of a grand jury, except in cases arising in the land or naval forces, or in the militia, when in actual service in time of war or public danger; nor shall any person be subject for the same offense to be twice put in jeopardy of life or limb; nor shall be compelled in any criminal case to be a witness against himself, nor be deprived of life, liberty, or property, without due process of law; nor shall private property be taken for public use, without just compensation." She was held for a crime by those representing the United States of America's interests without any sort of indictment, but her suit was denied thanks to the existence of such United States organized investigations as the Morgan Report.

Legally, such a court case could end up becoming a major legal quagmire. For example, an argument could be made in agreement with Lili'uokalani as she did not actually sign her legal name at the time. Then again, that same fact could be used against her by saying that she was aware that marrying under Christian traditions would make her subject to claiming the name of "Lili'uokalani Dominis" as she had been affectionately known that for quite some time. There is no way to tell. As it often happens, money makes the world go around and those with money are often the ones in control.

Thus ended the reign of the monarchy and the existence of the Kingdom of Hawaii as it had been previously known. Thus ended, in 1917, the life of a beautiful soul that was a friend, a confidant and a beloved Queen to the people of the Hawaiian Islands. Like a single flame of a candle dancing in the wind, long live the legacy of Queen Lili'uokalani!

Aftermath

Not much is known about Queen Lili'uokalani between 1899 and 1917 (during which time she withdrew from public life) other than the songs and stories that she wrote as well as the children's trust fund she had established in her name. She lived out her days in Washington Palace. She passed away in November of 1917 from complications following a stroke at the age of seventy-nine. Midnight of the evening she passed, her body was taken from her home to Iolani Palace. The rumble of thunder that occurred as she was laid in the room was seen as a good omen. She was later taken to the Kawaiaha'o Church at midnight the next evening. Her body remained there for seven days and then was transferred by royal procession to the Royal Mausoleum.

It was reported that her health had been poor many months prior to her death. Her death was described with intermittent moments of consciousness which eventually dissolved into a peaceful death. Her "true" people gathered together to mourn upon finding out about her death. By her side was Prince and Princess Kalanaiole, Colonel Lauhkea and his wife, and many other relatives. In addition to being the last monarch of Hawaii, she was also the last monarch buried with the ancient customs and rites of her people.

In 1903, Queen Lili'uokalani established a trust fund for Native Hawaiian children who were either orphaned or destitute. Though it could be used for any child in Hawaii falling under the same classification, she made it clear that the preference was for those of native blood. This trust was funded by her lands and other assets. Also, the Queen Lili'uokalani Children's Center was established in 1946 and has helped many families since that time.

Lili'uokalani brought a lawsuit against the United States government in 1910. She was seeking remuneration under the Fifth Amendment of the United States constitution. Her points were valid, but her lawsuit was quite unsuccessful. The actual records from this court preceding are not as widely available in any other source other than in legal libraries. Queen Lili'uokalani was seeking reparations and compensation for lost lands and other financial losses suffered due to her illegal compensation. Unfortunately, the court decided to agree with the Morgan report rather than Blount's account of his observations in regard to the legalities of the overthrow of the monarchy. Blount agreed with the Lili'uokalani, but his agreement meant that the Hawaiian Islands were foreign lands to the United States and the American sharecroppers would have to pay the tariffs on their exports. Because the court supported the Morgan report, which stated that the overthrow was legitimate and had legal basis, this meant that it supported the American sharecroppers in Hawaii in their efforts to reduce their shipping costs.

Speculation suggests that had the McKinley Tariff Act of 1890 had not been passed, the possibility exists that the overthrow of the Hawaiian monarchy might have never happened or might have happened much later in history. Though no one will ever know, the question will remain. Many laws enacted around that time changed history for the entire world. In a way, it could be seen that the American government betrayed the Hawaiian government as the Hawaiian government supported them during the time of the American Civil War. Still, greed and consumerism was the primary motive of the McKinley Tariff Act as well as the overthrow of the Hawaiian government and subsequent removal of the monarchy of the Kingdom of Hawaii.

Just as King Kamehameha the Great had a statue erected in his honor by one of his descendants, King Kamehameha V, Queen Lili'uokalani had one of her own likeness erected in 1982. A dedication brochure was created and in it, the statement reads about how Queen Lili'uokalani believed in the bond between a ruler and her people. It talks about how she defended her sovereignty.

After William Jefferson "Bill" Clinton assumed office in 1992, he had many different things on his proverbial plate. Around this time, it was brought to his attention that like the Native Americans, the Native Hawaiians' power of their own country was usurped by the United States government for profit and gain. Clinton, while in the process of making amends with other groups who also suffered egregiously at the hands of greed and corruption, sought to make amends with the Native Hawaiian people. So, in 1993, he signed the Apology Act which acknowledged the illegal overthrow of the Hawaiian monarchy and that the Hawaiians never actually gave up their claim to their government. This resolution or act was signed by President Bill Clinton on November 23, 1993.

Queen Lili'uokalani will always be remembered by her people as the "people's queen."

Author's Note

I hope you enjoyed my book on Queen Lili'oukalani. Writing it has been a labor of love. You may also enjoy my other book:

King Kamehameha The Great: King of the Hawaiian Islands

Made in United States
Cleveland, OH
27 November 2024

10885948R10026